RSPB first book of
birds

Anita Ganeri and **David Chandler**

A & C BLACK
AN IMPRINT OF BLOOMSBURY
LONDON NEW DELHI NEW YORK SYDNEY

Published 2011 by A&C Black,
An imprint of Bloomsbury Publishing Plc
50 Bedford Square, London WC1B 3DP
www.bloomsbury.com

ISBN: 978-1-4081-3718-5

Printed in China by C & C Offset Printing Co., Ltd.

A&C Black uses paper produced from elemental
chlorine-free pulp, harvested from managed
sustainable forests.

10 9 8 7 6 5 4

Contents

Birds

Birds are everywhere! Wherever you are, you can see them from your window or outside, even if you live in a big city. They are easy to see and fun to watch.

This book will help you name most of the birds you see around you. It also tells you about what they do and where they like to live. Find out which bird collects acorns. And which bird swallows stones!

At the back of this book is a Spotter's Guide to help you remember the birds you spot. You could also write down the birds you see, or draw them. Don't forget to listen to them too.

Turn the page to find out all about birds!

 # Robin

Robins are easy to find. They have orange faces and chests. They live in woods, parks and gardens. Robins sing all year round to keep other robins away from their homes.

Orange face

In winter, robins puff up their feathers to keep warm.

Orange chest

Baby robins are brown with spotty fronts.

They eat worms, seeds and fruit.

Blue tit

Blue tits have yellow breasts and bright blue caps. They live in gardens, parks and woods. Sometimes they hang upside down when they are feeding!

Blue tits eat insects, spiders, seeds, nuts and fruit.

Blue cap

Yellow breast

They lay eggs in holes in trees, or in nestboxes.

Great tit

Great tits are bigger than blue tits. They have a black stripe down their bellies. A male has a thicker black stripe than a female. Great tits live in woods, parks and gardens.

Great tits eat insects, nuts and seeds.

Black head with white cheeks

Green back

Listen out for their 'teacher teacher' song.

Black stripe down the front

Buzzard

A buzzard is a large bird of prey. Look out for it soaring high in the sky or perched on a fencepost. It can fly for a long time without flapping its wings.

Wing-tips open like fingers

Buzzards eat voles, rabbits, birds, insects and worms.

Broad wings

Short tail often spread like a fan.

They have sharp eyes for spotting prey.

Kestrel

The kestrel is a falcon. Watch out for it hovering over grass near roads. It is looking for food. Kestrels eat lots of mice and voles.

Kestrels sometimes live in cities.

Long pointed wings

Long tail

Some kestrels use the old nests of crows and other birds.

Male has grey tail with black band

Puffin

A puffin spends most of its life out at sea. It has a big beak. In summer, its beak turns bright red, blue and yellow. It has black wings and a white breast. It has orange feet and legs.

Puffins lay their eggs in burrows at the tops of cliffs.

Black and white head

They swim underwater to catch fish in their beaks.

Colourful beak

Bright orange legs and feet

Oystercatcher

You can see oystercatchers on the coast and by lakes and rivers. They have a long red beak for sticking into the mud and sand. They eat shellfish and worms.

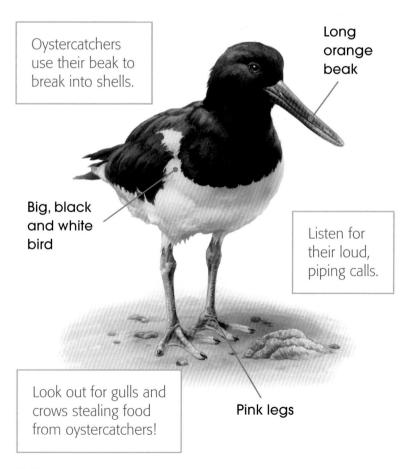

Oystercatchers use their beak to break into shells.

Long orange beak

Big, black and white bird

Listen for their loud, piping calls.

Look out for gulls and crows stealing food from oystercatchers!

Pink legs

Mallard

Mallards are easy to find.
They are a type of duck.
A male has a green
head and neck and
a blue patch on his wing.
A female is mostly brown.
Watch them tip up in
the water to feed.

They eat
seeds, plants,
insects and
shellfish.

Dark green
head and neck

Only female
ducks quack!

Brown chest

Shiny
blue wing
patch

13

Canada goose

These are big birds. You can see flocks of them near lakes and in parks. They honk loudly. Look out for them flying in a V-shape in the sky.

Males and females look the same, but the male is bigger.

White cheeks and chin

Long black neck

Mostly brown body

A group of geese on the ground is called a gaggle.

Mute swan

A mute swan is a huge bird. It lives on lakes, rivers and canals. It needs a lot of space to take off and land. The male has a bigger black bump on its beak than the female.

A mute swan swallows stones to help grind up its food.

White feathers

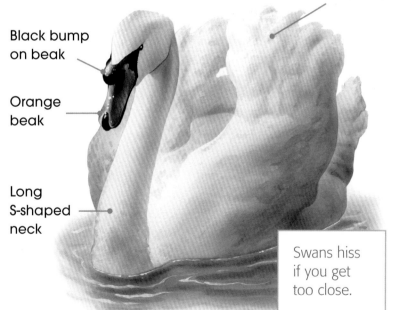

Black bump on beak

Orange beak

Long S-shaped neck

Swans hiss if you get too close.

Cygnets (baby swans) have grey-brown feathers.

House sparrow

You can see house sparrows in towns, cities, parks and gardens. They like to live near people. You could help house sparrows by putting up a nestbox, or planting flowers in your garden to attract insects for them to eat.

House sparrows eat seeds, berries and insects.

Black bib

Brown and black feathers

This picture is a male. The female has a brown head, with no head markings or black bib.

Magpie

Magpies are large, noisy birds that are easy to see. Listen for their loud 'chack-chack' call. Sometimes the light makes their wings and tail look blue or green.

Sometimes magpies store food in holes in the ground.

Black and white feathers

Very long tail

They build big, dome-shaped nests.

Barn owl

Look for barn owls just before it gets dark. You might see one hunting over farmland or over grass by a road. Sometimes they make a loud, shrieking noise. Baby barn owls snore when they want to be fed.

White face

Barn owls can turn their heads to look backwards.

White underneath

Barn owls swallow their prey whole without chewing first.

Sandy-brown and grey

Tawny owl

Tawny owls are big owls that live in woods, parks and big gardens. They hunt at night and are hard to see. You might hear them hooting to each other. One bird calls 'too-whit' and the other answers 'too-woo'.

Baby owls are called 'owlets'.

Big, black eyes

Brown feathers

They have very good hearing for finding food in the dark.

Herring gull

You can see herring gulls at the seaside. Sometimes, you will also see them a long way from the sea! They are big and mostly grey and white.

Some herring gulls look for food at rubbish tips.

Yellow beak with red spot

Black-and-white wing tips

Hungry chicks peck the red spot on an adult's beak to be fed.

Pink legs

Grey heron

These birds have long necks and long legs. Look for them standing still by rivers and lakes. They can stand hunched up or with their neck stretched out. They are very good at fishing!

Grey herons use a toe like a comb to brush their feathers.

Adult has long black feathers on head

Long bill

Sometimes they eat frogs.

Long neck

Their nests are big and made of sticks.

Long legs

Great spotted woodpecker

A great spotted woodpecker is black and white with a red patch under its tail. It lives in woods but sometimes comes into gardens to feed. It drums its beak against a trunk instead of singing.

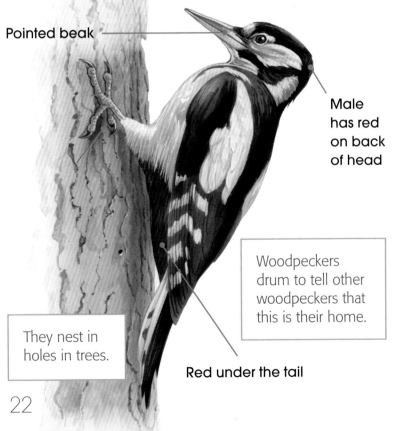

Pointed beak

Male has red on back of head

Woodpeckers drum to tell other woodpeckers that this is their home.

They nest in holes in trees.

Red under the tail

Cuckoo

Cuckoos are hard to see but you might hear one. They go 'cuck-oo, cuck-oo'. They lay their eggs in other birds' nests. These birds look after the young cuckoos.

Cuckoos live in many places including woods and moors.

Long tail

Pointed wings

Stripy chest

In Britain, you only see cuckoos in the spring and summer.

# Moorhen

Moorhens are dark-coloured waterbirds. They have a white line on their sides and white under their tails. If you see one walking, look at its long legs and toes.

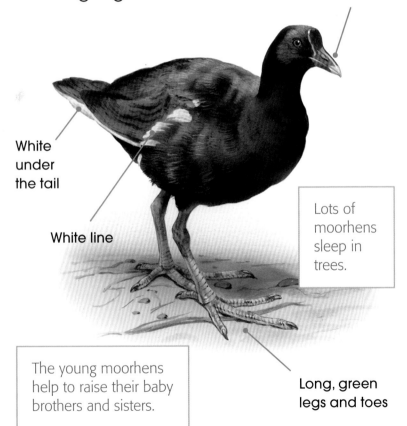

Red and yellow beak

White under the tail

White line

Lots of moorhens sleep in trees.

The young moorhens help to raise their baby brothers and sisters.

Long, green legs and toes

Coot

It is easy to get coots and moorhens mixed up. They are both waterbirds. A coot has a black body and a white beak and forehead. They are bigger than moorhens.

Look at a coot's toes. The flaps of skin help it swim.

Coots run on the water before they take off.

White beak and forehead

Black

Sometimes they steal food from swans and ducks.

Long legs and toes

Woodpigeon

This big pigeon often comes into gardens. Look for a white patch on its neck. When it flies, you can see a white stripe across its wings. As a woodpigeon flies out of a tree, its wings make a lot of noise!

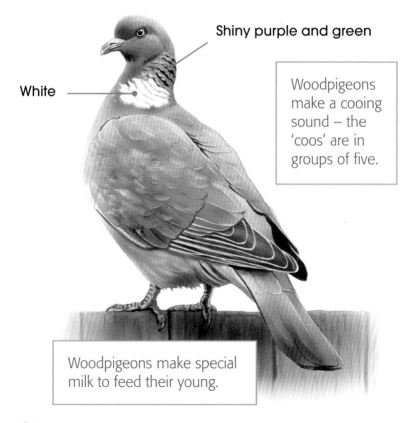

Shiny purple and green

White

Woodpigeons make a cooing sound – the 'coos' are in groups of five.

Woodpigeons make special milk to feed their young.

Collared dove

A collared dove is mostly pinkish-grey. It is smaller than a woodpigeon. Look for its black collar. It lives in gardens, parks and farms. You often see collared doves in pairs.

Collared doves make a cooing sound - the 'coos' are in groups of three.

Black collar

Dark wing tips

Thick white line down end of tail

Kingfisher

Kingfishers are small, and mostly blue and orange. Look for them flying low and fast over a river or lake. They dive underwater to catch fish with their long sharp beak.

Long, sharp beak

Kingfishers lay their eggs in burrows in river banks.

Female beak has orange on it. Male beak is all black.

Kingfishers eat fish, such as minnows and sticklebacks.

Blue and orange

Blackbird

Look for blackbirds feeding in the garden. They eat worms. The male is black with a yellow beak and yellow rings around his eyes. Females are brown.

Sometimes blackbirds grow some white feathers instead of black ones!

Yellow eye-ring

Yellow beak

Black

Watch a blackbird looking for food under leaves or listening for worms.

Wren

A wren is a tiny, brown bird with a big voice. Its tail sticks up. It lives in woods and gardens. It uses its beak to pick up insects to eat.

Some wrens eat tadpoles!

Tail sticks up

Short, rounded wings

A wren weighs less than a pencil.

Starling

A starling looks black but its feathers are really shiny purple and green. In the winter it has lots of white spots. It is often seen in the garden, eating insects and fruit.

Young starlings are brown.

Shiny black feathers

Short tail

Starlings can copy the songs of other birds.

Starlings are smaller than blackbirds.

Chaffinch

A chaffinch is a small but brightly coloured bird. The male is much more colourful than the female. They both have white markings on their wings. This picture is a male.

Grey

Pink

Chaffinches feed on insects and seeds on the ground.

White on wing

Green

When a chaffinch flies it shows a flash of white on its wings.

Greenfinch

The greenfinch is about the size of a chaffinch. Greenfinches come into gardens and feed on seeds and peanuts at bird feeders.

Greenfinches don't like sharing a bird feeder with other birds!

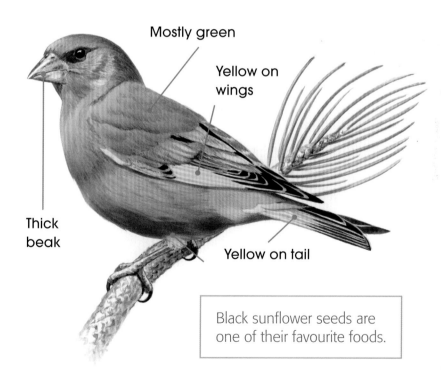

Mostly green

Yellow on wings

Thick beak

Yellow on tail

Black sunflower seeds are one of their favourite foods.

Carrion crow

Carrion crows are big and black. They are very clever birds. They smash seashells open by flying up and dropping them on rocks. Crows eat insects, seeds, fruit and dead animals.

Crows eat other birds' eggs and chicks.

Black feathers

Thick black beak

Crows are so clever that they can count!

Pied wagtail

A pied wagtail is a small, black, white and grey bird. It is easy to spot. Watch for it wagging its long tail up and down.

Pied wagtails mostly eat insects.

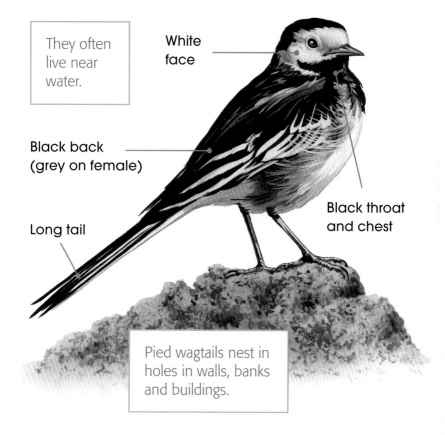

They often live near water.

White face

Black back (grey on female)

Long tail

Black throat and chest

Pied wagtails nest in holes in walls, banks and buildings.

35

 # Jay

Jays are big, colourful birds that live in woods. Sometimes they are seen in gardens. Listen for their loud, screeching call. In the autumn they are busy collecting acorns. This is a good time to see them.

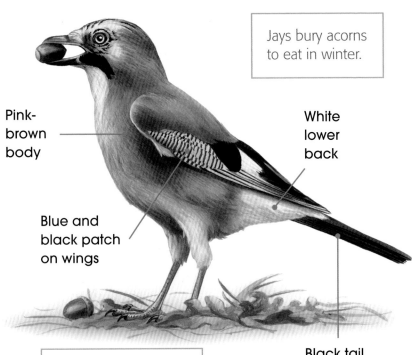

Jays bury acorns to eat in winter.

Pink-brown body

White lower back

Blue and black patch on wings

Black tail

They also eat insects, nuts and fruit.

Song thrush

Song thrushes live in woods, parks and gardens. They are very good singers. Song thrushes eat snails. They break the shells open by smashing them on stones.

Song thrushes sing the same thing over and over again.

Black spots

Brown

The spots on their front are shaped like upside down hearts.

Great crested grebe

Look for these birds on lakes. You might see them shaking their heads. This picture shows a bird in the summer. In the winter they don't have the fancy head feathers.

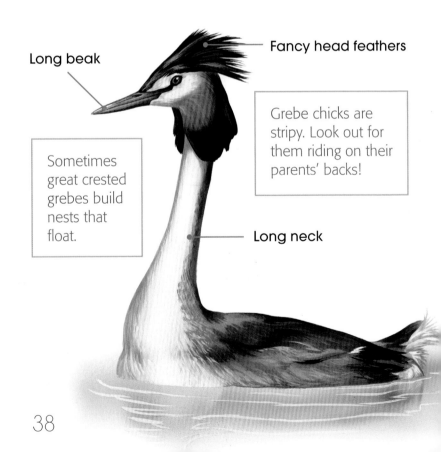

Long beak

Fancy head feathers

Grebe chicks are stripy. Look out for them riding on their parents' backs!

Sometimes great crested grebes build nests that float.

Long neck

Swift

In the summer, look in the sky to see swifts. They flap fast, then glide. When a young swift leaves the nest it flies non-stop for two or three years until it nests.

Swifts sleep as they fly.

They catch insects in the air.

Long, thin, curved wings

Pale throat

Mostly dark

Short forked tail

Swifts spend the winter in Africa.

Swallow

Swallows have forked tails with long streamers. Like swifts, swallows are fast fliers. Look out for them darting low over the ground and water with swept-back wings.

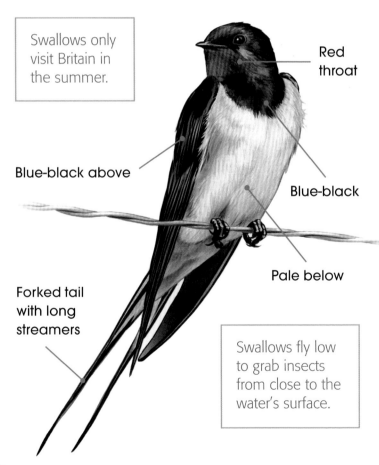

Swallows only visit Britain in the summer.

Red throat

Blue-black above

Blue-black

Pale below

Forked tail with long streamers

Swallows fly low to grab insects from close to the water's surface.

Useful words

bird of prey a bird that catches
 animals and birds for food

falcon a kind of bird of prey

forked split into two

gaggle a group of geese, usually
 on the ground

nestboxes small boxes for birds
 to nest in

owlets baby owls

prey creatures that birds of prey
 catch and eat

shellfish snails, cockles and mussels

voles wild mammals that look like
 small brown hamsters

Spotter's guide

How many of these birds have you seen? Tick them when you spot them.

Robin
page 6

Blue tit
page 7

Great tit
page 8

Buzzard
page 9

Kestrel
page 10

Puffin
page 11

Oystercatcher
page 12

Mallard
page 13

Canada goose
page 14

Mute swan
page 15

House sparrow
page 16

Magpie
page 17

Barn owl
page 18

Tawny owl
page 19

Herring gull
page 20

Grey heron
page 21

Great spotted
woodpecker
page 22

Cuckoo
page 23

Moorhen
page 24

Coot
page 25

Woodpigeon
page 26

Collared dove
page 27

Kingfisher
page 28

Blackbird
page 29

Wren
page 30

Starling
page 31

Chaffinch
page 32

Greenfinch
page 33

Carrion crow
page 34

Pied wagtail
page 35

Jay
page 36

Song thrush
page 37

Great crested
grebe
page 38

Swift
page 39

Swallow
page 40

Find out more

If you have enjoyed this book and would like to find out more about birds and other wildlife,  you might like RSPB Wildlife Explorers.

Visit www.rspb.org.uk/youth to find lots of things to make and do, and to play brilliant wildlife games.